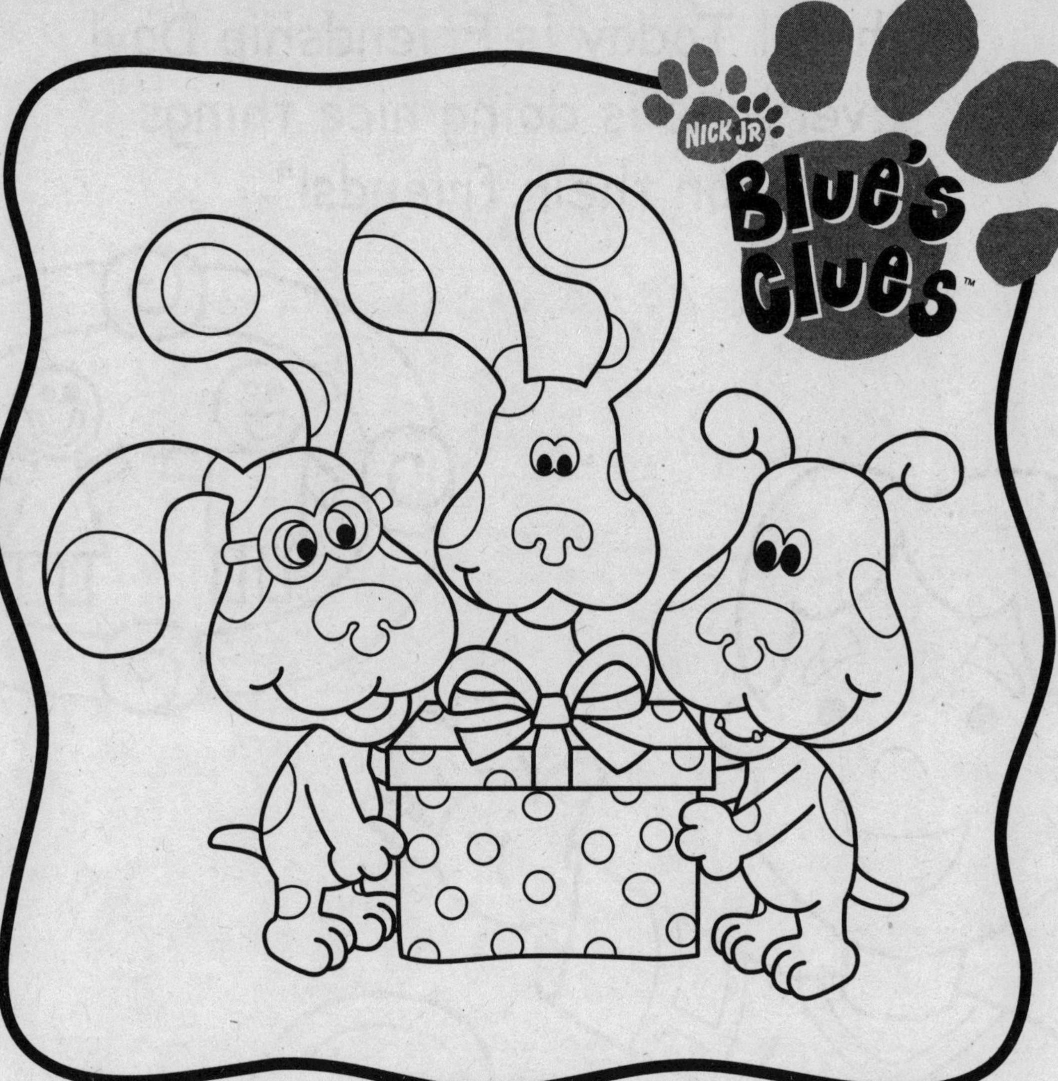

Blue's Friendship Day

Written by Astora Newton

Cover illustrated by Karen Craig
Interior illustrated by David B. Levy

A GOLDEN BOOK · NEW YORK

 Published in the United States by Golden Books, an imprint of Random House Children's Books, a division of Random House, Inc., New York, and simultaneously in Canada by Random House of Canada Limited, Toronto. Golden Books, A Golden Book, and the G colophon are registered trademarks of Random House, Inc. Blue's Clues, Nickelodeon, Nick Jr., and all related titles, logos, and characters are trademarks of Viacom International Inc.

ISBN: 0-307-10122-3

www.goldenbooks.com

Printed in the United States of America

10 9 8 7 6

"Oh, hi! Today is Friendship Day!
Everyone is doing nice things
for their friends!"

A present for a friend!

Mr. Salt made 2 matching cupcakes—
one for himself and one for Mrs. Pepper.
Will you circle the 2 cupcakes
that are the same?

At school, Magenta and Blue make a present
for Miss Marigold.

Magenta loves the color yellow.
Blue is giving her a marker for Friendship Day.
What color do you think it is?

What other yellow things might Magenta like?
Will you color them?

Will you help Magenta finish her pyramid drawing?
How many blocks go on the top?

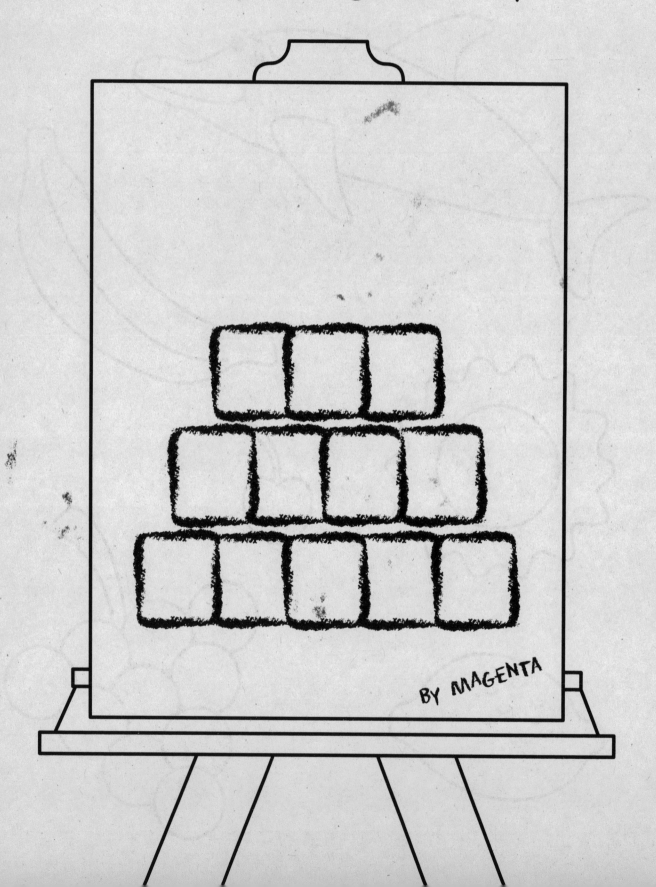

"What a nice present!"

A present for Magenta!
Which friend gave it to her?

Blue gave Magenta the picture!

Orange Kitten is making a card for her friend
Purple Kangaroo.

Will you help Orange Kitten decorate the card?
Finish the pattern along the sides!

Blue and Green Puppy put on a puppet show
for their friends!

Draw where you think the puppet show takes place!

Magenta gives her friend Blue a present!
What do you think it is?

It's a ball!

Purple Kangaroo shares his lunch
with his friend Magenta!

"I am making a necklace for my friend!
Guess who?"

Friends forever!

Hooray for Friendship Day!

Draw a picture for your friend!

A fort for everyone!

OUR FORT

"I'll mix the paint for the fort!"

GLUE

"A fort! Great idea, Blue!"

"We have all three clues!
Let's think. What could Blue want to build?"

Did you see the last clue?
Draw it in the Handy Dandy Notebook!

Periwinkle built a model spaceship for Joe!

Joe is building a city out of rocks!
Will you draw another building?

This spider is building a web!
Will you help finish it by drawing more lines?

Do you know what this bird is building?

Did you see the second clue?
Draw it in the Handy Dandy Notebook!

"I built this feeder for the birds!
If you see any birds, circle them!"

"We built this sand castle!"

Connect the ⬡s to see what Orange Kitten is building!

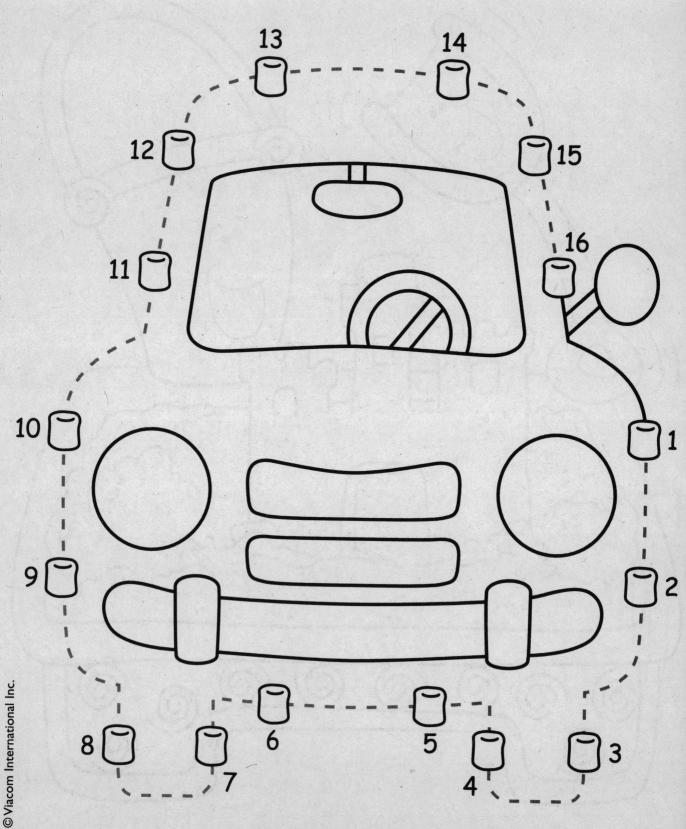

Orange Kitten is building something out of marshmallows and straws.

Help the Felt Friends build a bicycle by finishing the picture.

Can you guess what the Felt Friends are building?

Will you help Purple Kangaroo finish building his kite by drawing in the four sides?

Did you see the first clue?
Draw it in the Handy Dandy Notebook!

Cool hideout, Magenta!

Will you finish building Green Puppy's towers?
Continue the patterns!

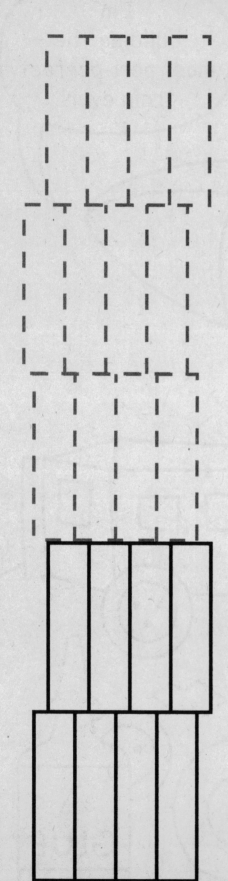

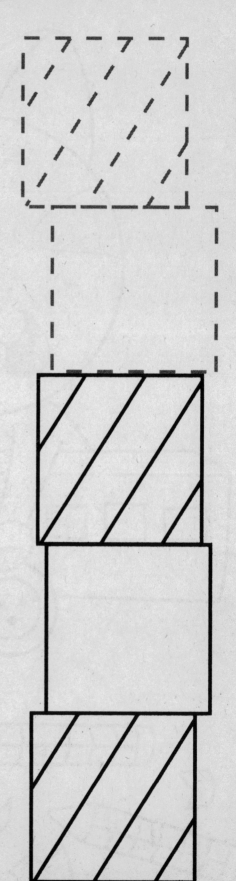

Green Puppy is building towers
with her blocks.

"Great idea!
Let's play Blue's Clues to figure out what
Blue wants to build!"

"What do you want to build, Blue?"

"Oh, hi! We're building stuff today.
Today is Building Day!"

What's Blue Building?

Written by Astora Newton

Cover illustrated by Karen Craig
Interior illustrated by David B. Levy

A GOLDEN BOOK · NEW YORK

ISBN: 0-307-10122-3

www.goldenbooks.com

Printed in the United States of America

10 9 8 7 6